Faith to Combat Every Setback

FAITH TO COMBAT EVERY SETBACK
I AM A FAITH FIGHTER

Erica Dees

© 2019 by Erica Dees

All rights reserved, including the right of reproduction in whole or in part in any form.

No part of this publication may be reproduced, stored in a retrieval system, or transmitted by any means without the written permission of the author.

Cover Design by Strongtower Photography and Graphics, www.sgdphotographics.com

ISBN: 978-0578570181

Printed in the United States of America. All rights reserved under international copyright laws.

Simon, Simon (Peter), listen! Satan has demanded permission to sift [all of] you like grain; but I have prayed [especially] for you [Peter], that your faith [and confidence in Me] may not fail; and once you have turned back again [to Me], strengthen and support your brothers [in the faith].
—Luke 22:31–32 (Amplified Bible)

To the individual struggling or desiring an increase in the area of faith. May every word you read impart the spirit of faith, and may you be empowered to both believe and receive the impossible as you are brought into an awakening of unshakeable, undeniable, and unfeigned faith!

TABLE OF CONTENTS

Introduction……………………………………………………..2

Chapter 1: The Fundamentals of Faith…………..4

Chapter 2: The Fight Faith Requires……………21

Chapter 3: Identity and Its Role in Faith………32

Chapter 4: The Proof Is in Your Walk—Now Walk It Out!………………………………………………..44

Chapter 5: Faith to Finish………………………………48

Bonus Chapter: Hallmarks of My "By Faith" Testimonies………………………………………………….52

Acknowledgments……………………………………….56

Introduction

I struggled to write this book until now. I realize that while writing this book, I was not only telling my story, but I was also telling the story of countless millions of those who've had a daunting experience with a setback. I received prophetic words that I would write several books, but those words remained a distant utterance that would someday be realized. I thought to myself, My life seems to be in shambles, so why would God ask me to share anything with anyone? I'm broken, headed to divorce court, and overwhelmingly confused about the life God promised and the one I am somehow living. I later learned that God was teaching me transparency in this place—something I struggled with, because I knew the judgment of men and how they could somehow excuse their own mishaps but openly criticize and condemn yours! Now because I am a counselor, and I promote accountability, I must admit that I equally battled pride. I did not want anyone to know that I was not as well as I portrayed. I wore shame as a garment with an underlay of bitterness, anger, and other emotions. Little did I know God was delivering me, healing me, and preparing me to be used for greater glory.

As children of God, it is imperative that we understand His principles. As we understand and apply these godly principles, we will avoid wasting time, talents, and treasures on things that do not satisfy. We will also understand that man's way of promoting could very well be God's way of demoting, and man's way of demoting could be God's way of promoting. Isaiah 55:8–9 (AMP) states, "For My thoughts are not your thoughts, nor are your ways My ways, declares the Lord. For as the heavens are higher than the earth, so are My ways higher than your ways and My thoughts higher than your thoughts."

~Chapter 1~
The Fundamentals of Faith

In our opening chapter, I wish to provide a foundation on which we will build subsequent ones. As would any good carpenter, I endeavor to skillfully present each piece of information and/or revelation to ultimately build *you* as a house of faith. I can recall it so vividly: I was sitting at my computer attempting to prepare a message on faith when suddenly I realized I didn't have enough information, and I certainly lacked the revelation to complete this task. I began asking God to give me a download, and this is what He said: "Faith is heaven's conduit that releases my promises unto you." I immediately searched for the definition of conduit and discovered that it is a channel or transport by which liquid or fluid flows. In Hebrews 11, when faith is mentioned, the transport words *by* and *through* are also used, which further substantiates this definition. Hebrews 11:2–3 (King James Version): "For by it [faith] the elders obtained [to get, acquire, secure, possess] a good report. Through faith we understand that the worlds were framed by the word of God, so that things which are seen were not made of things which do appear." From these passages, we can clearly see faith acting as the receptor (receiver) that allows oneness between heaven and earth. Just as turning on Wi-Fi allows access to internet services, so does faith in action allow access to heavenly promises. As much as we would desire, God is not going to leave His throne in order to place in our hands what we are believing Him for. Romans 10:6–10 (KJV): "But the righteousness which is of faith speaketh on this wise, Say not in thine heart, Who shall ascend into heaven? (that is, to bring Christ down from above:) Or, Who shall descend into the deep? (that is, to bring up Christ again from the dead.) But what saith it? The word is nigh thee, even in thy mouth, and in thy heart: that is, the word of faith, which we preach; That if thou shalt confess [say] with thy mouth the Lord Jesus, and shalt believe in thine heart that God hath raised him from the dead, thou shalt be saved. For with the heart man believeth unto righteousness; and with the mouth confession is made unto salvation." This Scripture is predominantly used to lead people into salvation; however, it equally reveals a principle of how, through faith, we gain access to heavenly realms where earthly requests are housed.

Faith in Its Spiritual State

According to John 4:24 (KJV), "God is a spirit: and they that worship him must worship him in spirit and in truth." This text outlines *how* communication with God happens spirit to spirit. Because faith is supernatural, we can conclude that when we are operating in faith, our faith is communicating with God spirit to spirit. Oftentimes our natural mind is trying to make logical sense of what can only be perceived by the spirit. Hence, it is imperative to remain in a spiritual state, because faith is productive in the spirit. It doesn't take a lot of effort to think and ultimately talk yourself out of something God has set in motion for your life. Jesus said, "The words that I speak, they are spirit, and they are life." Please be mindful of your speech! If the words you are speaking are not within these parameters (spirit and life), then do yourself a favor and refuse to speak.

2 Corinthians 4:13 (KJV): "We having the same spirit of faith, according as it is written, I believed, and therefore have I spoken; we believe, and therefore speak."

1 Corinthians 12:9 (KJV): "To another faith by the same Spirit; to another the gifts of healing by the same Spirit."

Galatians 5:22–23 (KJV): "But the fruit of the Spirit is love, joy, peace, longsuffering, gentleness, goodness, faith, meekness, temperance: against such there is no law."

Faith Operates in Truth

The Holy Spirit, who is also known as the spirit of truth, provides the parameters (boundaries) for our faith. He navigates our faith into the truth or reality of what is already ours. He would never have us believing God for something that is totally off limits! Though He would not, an unsubmitted will or desire could be an open door for the enemy to enter, masquerading as an answer to a prayer. This can be readily identified in the New Age culture as the law of attraction, which is the ability to attract into our lives whatever or whomever we are meditating or focusing on. I know some of you are asking, "Isn't this a biblical principle?" If this is your question, you are absolutely right. As with most occultic practices, it derives from biblical principles. Joshua 1:8 (KJV): "This book of the law shall not depart out of thy mouth; but thou shalt *meditate* therein day and night, that thou mayest observe to do according to all that is written therein: for then thou shalt make thy way prosperous, and then thou shalt have good success." It is important to note that God provided parameters and boundaries for Joshua when He said, "This book of the law." No offense, but self-help books do not substitute for the word of God. They may supplement, but they cannot serve as a substitute.

For this reason, I have purposely inundated this book with Scripture. Did you know that the word meditate translated in Hebrew means to moan, utter, or *speak*? Our meditation should reflect the word, either the *logos* (written) or *rhema* (spoken). After reflection, we should literally speak out what we read or heard either through the word of prophecy found in the Bible or through the spirit of prophecy, which comes by way of direct revelation from God through a dream, vision, impression, word of knowledge, word of wisdom, or a vessel. Now meditation can be and often is achieved through silence. This is not a bad practice, but sensitivity is encouraged. We must be aware of who or what is influencing our meditation. As stated in Scripture, the enemy has the power to transform himself into an angel of light. Why does this strike us as a surprise, when he was once an archangel? In Ezekiel 28:14, he's identified as the anointed cherub who stood and covered the very presence of God until one day iniquity was found in him. His fall is recorded in Isaiah 12:12–14. I invite you to study these Scriptures extensively if you haven't already. His desire and will was perverted as he desired to be like the Most High. Jealousy entered his heart, and he was no longer satisfied with his position, but his heart was filled with lust and greed, which led to corruption and ultimately banishment from the presence of God.

Now there's no way I can say all of this without asking you to take a moment to reflect on both your will and desires. Are they purified? Have you submitted them to the Lord? If not, please take a moment to do so, because as you can see, an unsubmitted will or desire is an open target for the enemy and has the potential to taint your faith.

"A means does not justify an end." I heard this so clearly as I was upstairs in my home one time, preparing my son for bed. I thought, Whatever can this mean? I walked downstairs to grab my phone, as I noticed I had a missed call. The strangest occurrence was unmistaken and undeniable. I had a caller ID app that provided information about callers even if they did not authorize it. The caller ID read "Devil's Cult." The hairs on my arm stood all the way up, as my son and I were home alone. The most interesting part of the entire occurrence was that the call came from the exact nationally and internationally known prophet who had been conducting automated calls and leaving prophetic words that were spot on! I must be honest, I would at times get a hunch in my spirit redirecting me away from this ministry, but I was in a very desperate season of my life. I was separated and vulnerable, and I desperately desired to hear something that would provide a ray of hope for reconciliation in my marriage. I had no desire to begin life again alone. Nevertheless, during this time, the Holy Spirit taught me a valuable lesson surrounding the importance of both submitting my will and desires to Him and discerning the motives of others. I pray that you too will give attention to your will and desires and to the motives of those around you.

Now that we've covered the parameters of faith and how it operates in truth, you should be ready to discuss what I identify as the object of faith, the opposition of faith, and the obedience faith requires. Earlier I provided the definition given to me by the

Lord. At this junction, I would like to include how faith is defined in the Greek. *Pistis* is the Greek word for faith, and it reflects total trust, reliance, and confidence in God. This will become more useful as we dig into the object of faith.

The Object of Faith

An object is a person or thing to which a specified action or feeling is directed. As a result, the object or focal point of our faith is God. We are to have faith (total trust, reliance, and confidence) in God. We can have faith for things, but our faith must be rooted in Him. Do you recall the account of Jesus cursing the fig tree, commanding it to wither up and die from the roots? Interestingly enough, the disciples heard him speak to an inanimate object but seemingly struggled with the likelihood of His words coming to pass. His response was simple yet profound. He said to them, "Have faith in God." I find this most intriguing, because the Bible says, "And his disciples heard it," but Peter was the only one that spoke what he heard and saw. The other disciples both heard and saw, but they did not say. I believe that Jesus was using this as a teachable moment to encourage boldness, which is connected to speech, confidence, and appearance regarding what we hear and see. Of course, He also addressed doubt, because it would serve as a nemesis to future encounters. However, if you look at the verse following Jesus's response, "Have faith in God," there seems to be a theme with the word say. Mark 11:23 (KJV): "For verily I say unto you, That whosoever shall say unto this mountain, Be thou removed, and be thou cast into the sea; and shall not doubt in his heart, but shall believe that those things which he saith shall come to pass; he shall have whatsoever he saith." In one verse, the word say or saith is mentioned four times. Biblically speaking, the number four derives its meaning from creation. On the fourth day of that which is known as creation week, God completed the material universe by bringing into existence the sun, the moon, and the stars. Your words have creative power! Take some time to reflect on this verse and say what you saw, to *see* what you *said*!

Scriptures that reflect God as the object of our faith include 1 Corinthians 2:5, 1 Peter 1:21, and Acts 3:16.

The Opposition of Faith

There are both extrinsic and intrinsic obstructions to faith, but for the sake of this session, I would like to specifically focus on the intrinsic obstructions. Intrinsic obstructions are the negative thoughts, feelings, and behaviors arising from within that serve as a barrier to belief (faith). Mark 7:15 (New Living Translation): "It's not what goes into your body that defiles you; you are defiled by what comes from your heart." In this text, Jesus was reproving religious leaders who were calling his disciples out for breaking their handwashing tradition. While they demanded adherence to a tradition, Jesus began shedding light on the true conditions of their hearts.

Moment of truth: I've been both a witness of and participant in religious dogma. And I must admit, there is nothing worse than being in relationship with someone of this sort. They are often well versed in Scripture but unfruitful in other areas such as love and life. This is so far removed from the Jesus model, because He is love, He is life, and He is exceptionally relational! Here's where I would like to list a few intrinsic obstructions to faith. I'm sure you've grasped the concept by now, so feel free to make this personal. You may record and discard the ones you've identified in yourself. Please note the following:

- Doubt
- Fear
- Unbelief

- Unforgiveness
- Lack of love
- Sin
- Jealousy
- Envy
- Bitterness
- Hatred
- Pride
- Slander
- Religious dogma

I asked you to record and discard because the moment we are presented with the truth, we become equally responsible to respond with a decision. Repentance (a decision to change one's mind) happens as a result of being faced with truth. Faith is so significant to God that upon His return, He will look for it in the earth. Luke 18:8 (NLT): "I tell you, he will grant justice to them quickly! But when the Son of Man returns, how many will he find on the earth who have faith?" Obviously, the earth here means the world, but did you know that we are also considered as earth and our hearts as soil? In 2 Corinthians 4:7 (NLT), we read, "We have this treasure in earthen vessels that the excellency of the power may be of God and not of us." Presently speaking, when God comes to answer our prayers, He looks first in our earth, our vessels, for faith. When our prayers and faith are not aligned, we experience a delay; however, when faith is present, it then becomes our proof of purchase, which results in answered prayers. Mark 11:24 (KJV): "Whatsoever things you desire when you pray, believe that you receive and you shall have them."

The Obedience Faith Requires

We will never experience the fullness of God apart from obedience. In fact, some promises are contingent upon our willingness to obey. Isaiah 1:19

(KJV): "If you be willing and obedient, you shall eat the good of the land." Hebrews 11:8 (KJV): "By faith Abraham, when he was called to go out into a place which he should after receive for an inheritance, obeyed; and he went out, not knowing whither he went." Abraham obeyed without having details. Are details trumping your obedience? If so, I admonish you to discard the need for more information and decide to obey. For some of you, this may be as simple as fasting, apologizing to someone although you were not at fault, or making some changes to your diet. I do not know what He is telling you to do, but whatever it is, do it! It takes faith to obey, but rest assured that while outcomes may not be clear to you, they are obvious to God. See Hebrews 11:7 (KJV) and Luke 5:3–6 (KJV).

~Thoughts from Chapter 1~

~Chapter 2~
The Fight Faith Requires

Fight the good fight of faith, lay hold on eternal life, whereunto thou art also called, and hast professed a good profession before many witnesses.
—1 Timothy 6:12 (KJV)

I imagine you had no idea the costs associated with believing God. I get it. Neither did I. When you believe God for something not visible to the human eye, your actions look ridiculously strange and somewhat annoying to the unbelieving. You make moves on the word while others mourn over the word. In Noah's day, God made a sovereign decision to destroy the earth. He was displeased with how man had become increasingly wicked as every imagination of their heart was set out to do evil. He identified that they had no plans to change, so He shared his plans for change with Noah, and instead of mourning over what God said, Noah moved. Genesis 6:8:

"But Noah found grace in the eyes of the Lord." The Amplified Version says, "Noah found favor and grace in the eyes of the Lord." Did you know that preservation (protection) comes with favor, and it is connected to righteousness? Psalm 5:12 (New International Version) says, "Surely, Lord, you bless the righteous; you surround them with your favor as with a shield." And in Job 10:12 (KJV), we read, "Thou hast granted me life and favor, and thy visitation hath preserved my spirit." As we walk in right standing with God, beholding His face, which is synonymous with His presence, we also increase in favor.

Luke 2:52 (AMP) says, "And Jesus kept increasing in wisdom and in stature, and in favor with God and men." I declare this over you right now! You will increase in wisdom and in stature, and you will have favor with God and men! Humanly speaking, Noah could have mourned over the word and chosen not to move for fear of being criticized by family and peers. After all, there was no physical evidence that a flood was coming. Noah's conversation with God was just between him and God. There were no witnesses to confirm what God had spoken; neither did God entrust this insight to anyone else. Are you waiting for someone to confirm what God has spoken to you in private? Confirmation is essential in certain stages of our development, but as we grow in relationship with God, we should reach a place of maturation where we trust His voice and move irrespective of man's consensus. When God speaks, you don't need evidence, because His word will be evident!

A War of Words

In case you are not aware, faith requires a fight. In fact, the apostle Paul instructed Timothy, his mentee, to fight; however, he was unequivocal in communicating the type of fight he needed to engage in. Understanding the type of fight you are in, as well as knowing your opponent, are critical components to winning. More often than not, we engage in meaningless battles only to lose the war. Must

I remind you that the weapons of your warfare are not carnal? The Greek word for carnal is *sarkikos*, which means the fleshly/worldly nature. It means simply being led by the flesh rather than the spirit. Galatians 5:16 (KJV): "This I say then, Walk in the Spirit, and ye shall not fulfill the lust [desires] of the flesh." Getting someone told, engaging in power struggles, or making decisions based on fleshly desires are sure ways to lose the war. Nevertheless, I am not tasked with teaching you how to lose. If you are reading this book, I'm quite sure you've had some losses, which have invoked an inner determination to win at all cost. So let's embark upon your next win, shall we? Prophetically speaking, the faith fight will drastically increase as we draw closer to the end times. We will inevitably face global and political oppositions that will test the very core of who we are and what we believe. Jude 1:3 (KJV) warns, "Beloved, when I gave all diligence to write unto you of the common salvation, it was needful for me to write unto you, and exhort you that ye should earnestly contend for the faith which was once delivered unto the saints." When God releases a word in our life, it is our responsibility to respond in faith and contend with the word until we see it manifest. Most times, people experience resistance en route to manifestation and shrink down as opposed to fighting back. In 1 Peter 5:9 (AMP) we read, "But resist him, be firm in your faith [against his attack—rooted, established, immovable], knowing that the same experiences of suffering are being experienced by your brothers and sisters throughout the world. [You do not suffer alone.]" If God has given you a promise concerning your family, finances, health, education, ministry, or business and you're seeing the opposite of that promise, keep contending. If it's not good yet, then God is not done. He will not stop until you are brought into the fullness of His plans for your life. Jeremiah 29:11 (NLT) reminds us, "'For I know the plans I have for you,' says the

Lord. 'They are plans for good and not for disaster, to give you a future and a hope.'"

I am giving these instructions with the assumption that you have received the word of the Lord concerning your situation. If this is not the case, I encourage you to devote time to the word until you receive a word, or to get around prophetic people that will help activate you in the hearing and sensing realm, as hearing is the prerequisite for believing. Romans 10:14 (English Standard Version) asks, "How then will they call on him in whom they have not believed? And how are they to believe in him of whom they have never heard? And how are they to hear without someone preaching?" And Romans 10:17 (New King James Version) says, "So then faith comes by hearing and hearing by the word of God."

In chapter 1, I outlined the fundamentals of faith, providing clear principles and basic teachings relative to faith. Throughout this chapter, I will be highlighting how a vast majority of the faith fight involves what I would describe as a "war of words." It is the place where your words are scrutinized to determine changes in your confession. You are only proven a reliable witness when your confession remains the same. What you believe must be consistent with what you confess (say). So in casual conversations or moments when you are tempted to fear, you must be intentional with your words. It is your words, not the words of another, that discredit your reliability as a witness and therefore delay your prophetic promise. Proverbs 6:2 (NIV) tells us, "You have been trapped by what you said, ensnared by the words of your mouth." Recall Zechariah's encounter with the angel Gabriel while he was carrying out his assignment in the temple (Luke 1:18–19, NLT): "Zechariah said to the angel, 'How can I be sure this will happen? I'm an old man now, and my wife is also well along in years.' Then the angel said, 'I am Gabriel! I stand in the very presence of God. It was he who sent me to bring you this good news! But now, since you didn't believe what I said, you will be silent and unable to speak until the child is born. For my words will certainly be fulfilled at the proper time.'"

When God sends your answer in seed form, do not underestimate its potency, power, and potential. Seed in the Bible is synonymous to the word. See Luke 8:11 (NIV): "This is the meaning of the parable: The seed is the word of God." In the natural world, if a woman receives seed from a man during her time of ovulation (when she's most fertile), she can conceive. If you are going to break cycles, as they can only be broken through a seed, then you need the right word along with the right response.

I pray that we would walk in a more profound revelation of the power of our words. Gabriel understood this very well, as angels are signaled by the word. Psalm 103:20 (NKJV): "Bless the Lord, you His angels, who excel in strength, who do His word, heeding the voice of His word." The Bible also states that after three weeks of fasting and praying, Daniel encountered the angel Gabriel, who said, "I am come in response to your words" (Dan. 10:12, New American Standard Bible). In one instance the Bible depicts Gabriel heeding the voice of God, and in another instance we see him responding to the words of a man. When we speak the word, we give voice to it and therefore signal the response of angels. Hence, Zechariah was silenced by Gabriel because his words had the potential to initiate unnecessary warfare, thus delaying the promise. The next time you are tempted to make a confession opposite of what you originally believed, remember your rights. You have the right to remain silent. Anything you say can and will be used against you in the courts of heaven. Remember Revelation 12:10–11 (NKJV): "Then I heard a loud voice saying in heaven, 'Now salvation, and strength, and the kingdom of our God, and the power of His Christ have come, for the accuser of our brethren, who accused them before our God day and night, hast been cast down. And they overcame him by the blood of the Lamb and by the word of their testimony, and they did not love their lives to death.'"

~Thoughts from Chapter 2~

~Chapter 3~
Identity and Its Role in Faith

For I say, through the grace given unto me, to every man that is among you, not to think of himself more highly than he ought to think, but to think soberly, according to as God hath dealt to every man the measure of faith.
— Romans 12:3 (KJV)

I remember when I was separated from my husband and how I longed for reconciliation. I lay in my bed not knowing what I would face in the days to come. While I lay there, I had a vision of my driver's license lying on the floor face down. I had to do a double take to ensure it wasn't really on the floor and that my eyes were not playing tricks on me, as the "old folks" used to say. I asked God for the interpretation of this vision, and He said, "Do not lose your identity!" As it was in the spirit world, so it happened in the natural one. I was faced with a situation that set me back, and I mean way back! Omniscient, all-knowing God prepared me for an encounter I had no idea would occur. During this time, I relied heavily on God, along with the prayers of a few trusted friends. I could literally feel my mind leaving, so in dread and utter desperation, I called out to God, "Please don't let me lose my mind!" I quickly recalled His words: "Do not lose your identity!" And I remembered Proverbs 25:11 (KJV): "Like apples of gold in settings of silver is a word spoken at the right time." At this moment, I was given a window of grace to choose life over death. Clearly, I chose life, but this encounter resulted in me becoming more cognizant of the enemy's tactic to create distorted realities. Hence, I deemed it necessary to dedicate an entire chapter to identity and its role in faith.

What You Think Affects What You See and Ultimately What You Believe

In Romans 12:3, our opening Scripture, the writer provides clear directives as to how we should and should not think. He tells us not to think *more highly* of ourselves, but this should not be misinterpreted as not thinking of yourself highly. I love what Kris Vallotton says: "Humility is not thinking less of yourself, but rather thinking of yourself less." Low self-esteem and insecurity are not humility at all. They are the root of rejection that plagues individuals who lack identity. Self-perception (the way we see ourselves) plays a huge role in our relationship with God as well as others. People with the wrong perception of themselves have a proclivity (tendency) to shy away from intimate relationships, sabotage developing ones, or attribute negative thoughts and feelings to the people they are in relationship with. As clinicians, we characterize this as projection. Projection is a defense mechanism that occurs when an individual attributes a characteristic they find unacceptable in themselves onto another.

Journey with me into the account of the spies that brought back an evil report after being commissioned by God through Moses to spy on the promised land. Numbers 13:33 (KJV): "And there we saw the giants, the sons of Anak, which come of the giants: and we were in our own sight as grasshoppers, and so we were in their sight." Please allow me to draw your attention to several truths concerning the spies and to elaborate on each.

1. God had already given them the land; they only needed to possess it.
2. They were *all* leaders.
3. The way they perceived themselves reflected how they perceived God and therefore how they felt their opponents perceived them.

If you read the preceding verses, you will find God's original plan conveyed in His conversation with Moses (Num. 13:1–2, KJV): "And the Lord spake unto Moses, saying, Send thou men, that they may search the land of Canaan, which I give unto the children of Israel: of every tribe of their fathers shall ye send a man, every one a ruler among them." God clearly states that he had given the land unto the children of Israel. He was not asking them to go after something they had no rights to. It was theirs; they just needed the right strategy to possess it—but God even had that covered! His strategy was for them to first spy on the land. A spy is a person who secretly collects and reports information on the activities, movements, and plans of an enemy. God's strategy included them having detailed knowledge of their opponents not to be intimidated by them, but to *defeat* them. Gone are the days where we echo myths such as "What you do not know will not hurt you."

The truth is what you do not know has the potential to destroy you, be it spiritually or naturally. Hosea 4:6 (KJV): "My people are destroyed for lack of knowledge." As believers, we filter sensual knowledge through the spiritual truth of His word, which then opens the door for revelation (the act of revealing, shedding light on, or communicating divine truth already existing but not yet revealed). In her book, *Rules of Engagement,* Dr. Cindy Trimm says, "Darkness is the absence of God, revelation, and purpose. When the light comes on, revelation shows up." As previously mentioned, these spies were called upon to spy on the land, which included the inhabitants of the land, the condition of the land, and the cities in the land. This knowledge was intended to serve as weapons in their conquest arsenal.

Conversely, because they had issues with their identity, they began casting an image upon themselves and the inhabitants of the land that totally removed God from the equation. They became paralyzed in fear instead of propelled by faith. This is particularly significant because they were heads of households and tribes, which is translated as leaders. By position alone, they had the power to influence and persuade, and by God, they did just that. If you read the succeeding chapter, you will find that after hearing the evil report of these leaders/influencers, their people group responded in disbelief, despair, despondency, disappointment, disarray, and ultimately rebellion (see Num. 14:1–12, NLT). If a leader lacks identity, he or she runs the risk of reproducing dysfunction and propagating falsehood to the people they lead. I hope that you are grasping the importance of identity and how it impacts faith. Has God given you something to possess, but you're magnifying (making something larger than it is) the opposition instead of amplifying (increasing the volume of) what He said? Simply turn up the volume of His words by reading, recalling, and rehearsing what He said and how He said it! The results are astounding!

Identity Lost and Found

All of this talk about identity but no precise definition. Well, here it is, the definition you've been waiting for! Identity can be described as the unique characteristics that make you an individual. It is who you are, what you possess, and where you are assigned. Since this is a faith-based book derived from biblical principles, it would be impossible for me to discuss identity without introducing its origination in God. In the book of beginnings, where creation is recorded, we read that God created man in His image after His likeness (who you are). He then gave him dominion, which is authority (what you possess), over the fish of the sea, the fowl of the air, and every living thing that moved upon the earth (where you are assigned). It is important to note that man had dominion on the earth over the fish of the sea, the birds of the air, and every living *thing*, not a person. I wonder what life would be like if we relinquished our efforts to exert authority over people and began dominating in the place and thing where we are assigned. Can you imagine a world where people have so enthralled themselves into purpose that their every action is purpose directed? There would be no wasted time, no wasted talents, and indeed no wasted treasures. The world without would both reflect and respond to the world within as *we* become conduits for the kingdom of God to flow in the earth!

In case I haven't made it clear, we are sons and daughters. We have a heavenly Father who is in love with us, and His every thought toward us is good. If you have an estranged relationship with your natural parents, you may struggle to receive this truth, but it is this truth that empowers you to walk in corresponding truths regarding faith and the like. If you've come to the realization that you've not been able to operate in faith because you've partnered with a false version of yourself, there is redemption for you! There are practical steps that you can take to reclaim your identity. Such steps include repentance (changing your mind and behavior), rehearsing Scriptures about sonship and the Father's love, inner healing, deliverance, and/or counseling. Personally, I have engaged in all of them. Someone asked me if I thought counseling was beneficial or even necessary for someone who is a believer. They asked, "Couldn't I just fast and pray my pain away?" I was so happy to provide them with an answer from an educational, spiritual, and experiential perspective. Fasting and praying are powerful spiritual disciplines and should be incorporated in the life of every believer. However, it is quite easy to become rigid and religious as opposed to relational in our approach, which yields no change. As we journey through life, we encounter people who have met others who have exposed them to some degree of hurt. This hurt, if not addressed, shapes our personality, develops toxic thinking patterns, and creates strongholds in our mind that we are often unaware exist. It is the work of a skilled counselor to give perspective by revealing the whys and whats so that we may apply new patterns of thinking, resulting in a healed mind.

~Thoughts from Chapter 3~

~Chapter 4~
The Proof Is in Your Walk—Now Walk It Out!

Have you heard the old saying, "The proof is in the pudding?" This saying simply implies that something can only be verified as truth after it has been experienced and proven. I am emphatically stating that the veracity of your faith is determined by your walk. I encourage you to think of walking in terms of actions, behaviors, conduct, and movement. We read in 2 Corinthians 5:7, "For we walk by faith, not by sight." It is in walking our faith that we can become weary. That's partly because we have placed God on a timeline, and when He does not act within the timeframe we've implemented, disappointment sets in. Psalm 105:19 (NLT): "Until the time came to fulfill his dreams, the Lord tested Joseph's character." Faith is now, but your walk of faith is progressive. The Bible says we go from faith to faith and from glory to glory.

While you're walking, God is developing character and consistency.

Will you remain committed and faithful if your prayer is not answered with whom or in the way you expected? There were times in my life that I honestly felt like life was happening without me. I did not see clearly the direction I was headed, and I had people tell me that you've got to have "blind faith." Now, I understood their hearts and what they were suggesting, but God revealed to me that there is no such thing as "blind faith." Faith knows precisely where it is headed, even when we are uncertain. It is impossible for you to walk by something that does not have a vision. Why would God tell us to walk by faith if faith were blind? And if the blind lead the blind, both shall fall into the ditch (Matt. 15:14, KJV). Faith takes us into the realm of the impossible, where revelation is necessary. In this realm, God removes scales from our eyes, conveying deep insights regarding His will (Eph. 1:15–19, AMP).

In the middle of the night, Jesus came walking on the sea. When the disciples saw it, they thought it was a ghost and responded in fear. Jesus spoke to their fear and extended an invitation for them to walk their faith out. Peter accepted and said, "Lord, if it's you, bid me come." Jesus said come, and Peter came (Matt. 14:29, KJV): "And he said, Come. And when Peter was come down out of the ship, he walked on water, to go to Jesus." Yes, Peter walked on water, but can I suggest that walking on the word gave him the power to walk on water? You are someone's proof, so walk it out!

~Thoughts from Chapter 4~

~Chapter 5~
Faith to Finish

When God was placing a demand on me to finish this book, I would see the Nike sign everywhere with an emphasis on "Just Do It!" I must admit, I was full of excuses as to why I could not "just do it," but none of my excuses mattered to God. He knew what He had equipped me with, regardless of how I felt. My own feelings of inadequacy had no reflection on Him and who He had predetermined me to be. More often than we would like to admit, we project our humanity, which is inundated with limitations and boundaries, onto God's divinity, which is limitless and immeasurable unto man; there's just absolutely no comparability between the two. Please review chapter 3, "Identity and Its Role in Faith," for a more in-depth look into how what we believe about ourselves affects what we believe about God. Getting back to the "just do it" mantra, has God commanded you as He had me to "just do it"? If you've answered yes, then it is time that you relinquish your need to control outcomes, release your desire to explore other options, and *just do it*! Do you know that finishing is congruent with the character and nature of God? In the book of beginnings, where the Creator created creation, we see rest as a byproduct of finishing (Gen. 2:1–2, KJV): "Thus the heavens and the earth were finished and all the host of them. And on the seventh day God ended his work which he had made, and he rested on the seventh day from all his work which he had made." Elohim, the God that creates, did not rest until He finished. Your restlessness could be an indicator that you have unfinished business. Recall the account of the child Jesus traveling with His parents and how He was later found lingering in the temple. His response to His anxious and worried mother was, "Did you not know that I must be about my father's business?" Whether you are a CEO, full-time employee, stay-at-home parent, or ministry leader, your first call is to be a good steward over the Father's business. His business is the kingdom, which speaks to His rule and reign over the earth. It is His right way of doing things, as well as His influence on a people or place. Inviting Him in our endeavors endows us with grace to finish.

We are presently living out a story that has already been written. Perhaps you're unaware of its ending—*we finish strong*! Hebrews 12:2 (KJV) tells us, "Looking unto Jesus the author and finisher of our faith; who for the joy that was set before him endured the cross, despising the shame, and is set down at the right hand of the throne of God." See also Philippians 1:6 (KJV).

~Thoughts from Chapter 5~

~Bonus Chapter~
Hallmarks of My "By Faith" Testimonies

1. By faith, Erica submitted a thirty-day notice to a job without the prospect of a new job and was later hired in a position with a company where she made thousands of dollars more.

2. By faith, Erica was approved for a new construction loan to build a home. Though previously approved, she was later denied by the builder's lender, only to have him contact her the next day to apologize and say he had to retract his decision of disapproval and reapprove the loan!

3. By faith, Erica, along with other prayer warriors, believed God would give her mom a new heart without surgery after she had been prepped for stent placement. The doctors later entered the room and announced that her mom's heart was healthy and a stent was not necessary. When an inquiry about her mother's blood pressure was made, the doctor responded, "Her blood pressure is better than mine!"

4. By faith, Erica received an unexpected check in the mail to cover event expenses in the days leading up to the event, providing the money she did not have!

5. This is hilarious but true: by faith, Erica spoke to a backed-up commode, which then unclogged itself,

saving hundreds of dollars by avoiding the need to call a plumber!

~Track with Me! What Is Your "By Faith" Testimony? ~

~Thoughts from the Book~

ACKNOWLEDGMENTS

I would like to first say thanks to my heavenly Father, who has entrusted me to deliver His message with the same power He delivered it unto me. I would also like to thank my earthly father, the late minister George Dees, for the time he spent imparting the word in me and for not allowing me to play as normal children played, though I so desperately desired it. He knew that there was something extraordinary about the call of God on my life, and it is that seed of the word that produced this book. I would like to honor my mother, Alfreda Dees, for believing in me when I did not believe in myself. It was your prayers, disciplinary actions, and refusal to allow me to accept life as it was that pushed me to be the woman I am today! I would like to acknowledge my sisters: Kathleen, Denise, Alfreda, and Necole. You guys know the pre- and post-Erica and yielded love, respect, and support throughout my process. I would like to say thanks to my God-given son, John Carter Pace: you are both heaven's and Mommy's most prized possession! I would like to recognize my tribe, Greg (Maeola) Coleman and Quinten (Siera) Howard: you guys did not allow me to lose sight of purpose when I felt I had lost me! I would like to express gratitude to Vonetta Parker for your continuous support and friendship, as well as your editing eye during early stages of production. I would like to show appreciation to my mentee and ministry colleague, Lakeisha Phillips, for seeing me as fruitful in a season where I counted myself as barren. I would like to acknowledge my semi-book coach, prayer partner, and confidant, Tracy Byars, for your unacceptance of anything less than what you knew to be true! I would like to say thanks to Yolanda Crowder, who is also a prayer partner and trusted friend and prayed this book into completion. I would like to extend gratitude to Apostle Patricia Slaughter for speaking this book into existence. And lastly, I would like to thank you for giving me a space in your world to release this message of faith!

www.ingramcontent.com/pod-product-compliance
Lightning Source LLC
Chambersburg PA
CBHW071415290426
44108CB00014B/1838